Industrial Growth in New York

Holly Cefrey

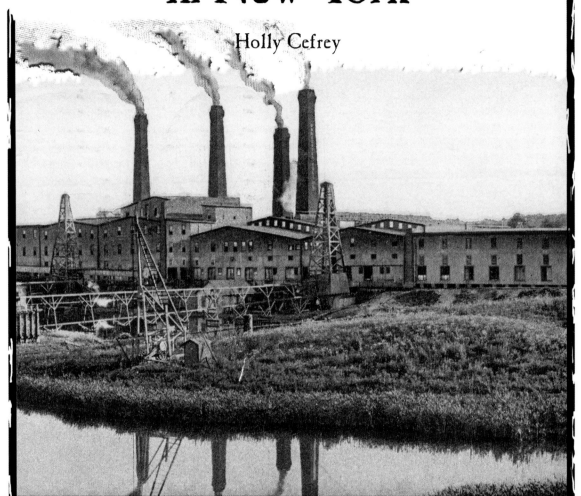

ROSEN CLASSROOM
PRIMARYSOURCE

Rosen Classroom Books & Materials

New York

Published in 2003 by The Rosen Publishing Group, Inc.
29 East 21st Street, New York, NY 10010

Book Design: Ron A. Churley

Photo Credits: Cover, pp. 1, 16 © Rykoff Collection/Corbis; p. 4 © Collection of New-York Historical Society; p. 8 © Lee Snider; Lee Snider/Corbis; pp. 10, 14, 20 © Corbis; pp. 12, 14 (inset) © Hulton/Archive; p. 12 (inset) © Rare Books & Manuscripts, New York Public Library; p. 16 (inset) © Independence National Historical Park; p. 18 © Schenectady Museum, Hall of Electrical History Foundation/Corbis; p. 18 (inset) Bettmann/Corbis.

ISBN: 0-8239-8409-5
6-pack ISBN: 0-8239-8421-4

Manufactured in the United States of America

CPSIA Compliance Information: Batch #WR112240RC: For Further Information contact Rosen Publishing, New York, New York at 1-800-237-9932

Contents

A Dutch Colony

New York state began as a Dutch trading region in the early 1600s. The Dutch chose the area because they could get animal furs from Native Americans in return for metal tools, cloth, and weapons. The animal furs were highly valued in Europe.

The region also offered other valuable **natural resources**, including trees for lumber, good soil for farming, and waterways filled with fish. Waterways were also important for travel, establishing trading ports, and shipping goods. The trading region became a Dutch colony when the first settlers arrived in 1624.

◀ This map of the northeast coast of America was made around 1685 by Dutch mapmaker Nicolaes Visscher II. It is a revised version of a map made around 1655. This map appeared in a book of maps that Visscher published around 1685.

A British Colony

England gained control of New Netherland in 1664. It was renamed New York in honor of King Charles II's brother James, the duke of York. The settlers followed English rule and paid taxes to England. England allowed local governments to make some of their own laws.

Albany was the only settlement given the right to carry on the fur trade. New York City became the only port where all goods were loaded or unloaded. Towns were settled in the valleys of the Hudson and Mohawk Rivers. Settlers built sawmills to turn trees into lumber. A hard-working settler could clear an **acre** of land in about ten days!

◀ Agriculture was the most important business during the colonial period in New York. About 80 percent of New Yorkers made their living by farming.

The Growing State

During the early 1800s, people from many countries **immigrated** to New York. The population grew quickly. Settlements in western New York needed a constant supply of goods, which they received from craftspeople, merchants, and traders in New York City. In return, farmers in the west sent produce to New York City.

This growth created new needs. New roads were needed to make **transportation** easier and faster. Products had to be made in large numbers to satisfy the needs of settlers. Businessmen such as Colonel Nathaniel Rochester did much to help New York grow. In the early 1800s, he founded the town of Danville on the Genesee River. Soon after that he founded the village of Rochester around gristmills he built on the Genesee River.

◀ Philipsburg Manor in Tarrytown, New York, was established by Frederick Philipse in the 1700s. It was an important water-powered gristmill in New York before the American Revolution. Farmers once used gristmills to grind grain into flour.

New York Finance

During the late 1700s and early 1800s, British manufacturers chose New York City as a place to unload goods. Thousands of merchants went to New York City to buy and sell goods from all over the world. New York gained control of trade across the Atlantic Ocean, along America's east coast, and with towns and cities that were further **inland**. Banks formed to help run the city's financial matters.

On May 17, 1792, local businessmen created the first New York **stock market**. The men agreed to buy and sell the **stocks** of different companies. This became the New York Stock Exchange.

◀ In 1784, a group of wealthy New Yorkers started the Bank of New York. By 1815, there were five banks in New York City. The banks were built in Manhattan on and near Wall Street, which is shown in this picture from 1869. After 1840, the banking activities of the entire nation were centered in New York City.

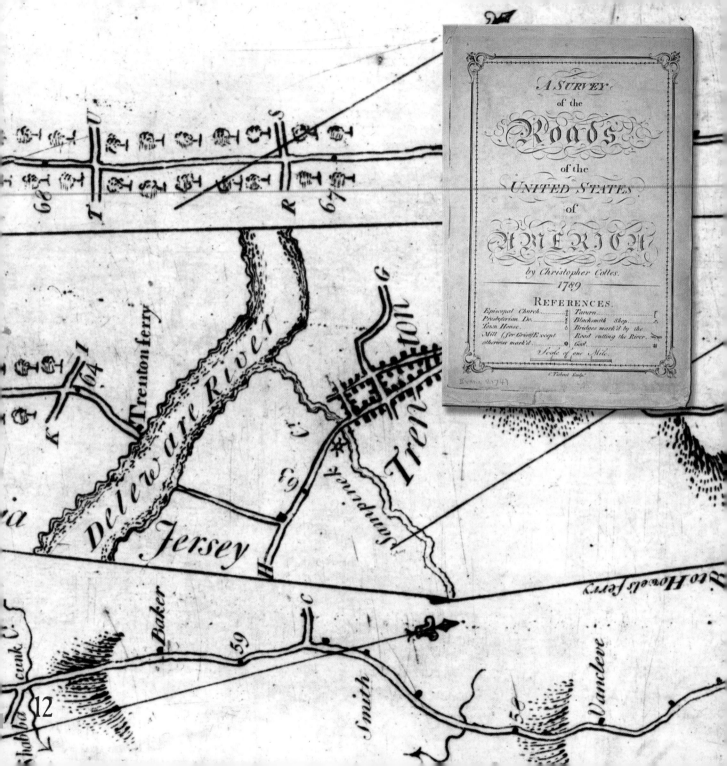

New Roads

New roads allowed farmers and communities to share in the wealth of New York state. Roads soon linked rivers and towns to major trade routes. New York's earliest roads were widened trails that had first been used by Native Americans. Traveling over these rough roads was not easy. **Turnpikes** and **plank** roads were built to make travel easier.

Between 1797 and 1807, 900 miles of turnpikes were built throughout New York state. By 1821, 278 turnpike companies had built 4,000 miles of roads in New York. Builders started making plank roads instead of turnpikes in the 1840s. The first plank road in New York was located north of Syracuse.

◀ Pictured here is the cover and a page from a book of road maps published in 1789 by Christopher Colles. Colles's book of maps was the first American road guide.

De Witt Clinton

The Erie Canal

In 1817, Governor De Witt Clinton broke ground for the Erie Canal in Rome, New York. It was completed in 1825. The canal joined the Great Lakes to the Atlantic Ocean. It was 363 miles long, forty feet wide, and four feet deep. The main canal had eighty-three locks.

The canal made transportation easier, faster, and less expensive. Inland trade helped New York become a major financial center. Manufactured goods were shipped westward to pioneers and western towns. Lumber and crops were shipped eastward to seaports. Before the canal was built, New York City was the nation's fifth largest seaport. By 1840, it had become the nation's largest seaport.

◄ The canal business employed thousands of New Yorkers and greatly reduced shipping costs. For example, the canal lowered the cost of shipping goods between Buffalo and Albany from $100 per ton to under $10 per ton! This painting of the Erie Canal is a copy of one that was created by John William Hill in 1829.

Robert Fulton

Inventions in Industry

Inventions of the 1800s contributed to the growth of **industry** in New York state. Railroads could ship items faster and farther than any other kind of transportation. It became easier to ship goods that could spoil quickly, like meat, across the state. Railroads allowed factories to grow more quickly. Large loads of coal could be sent to factories and businesses regularly. Coal was burned to heat the water used in steam systems. Steam systems powered the manufacturing machines. As early as 1846, factories in Utica were using steam to power machines used to make cloth. By 1860, nearly all parts of New York state had railroad service.

◀ In 1807, an inventor named Robert Fulton created the first successful steam-powered boat, the *North River* (later called the *Clermont*). Shown here is the first New York steam-powered passenger train, the De Witt Clinton. This train first traveled from Albany to Schenectady on August 9, 1831.

Factory Boom

By 1860, factories were built all over New York state to create goods in large amounts. Cotton factories were built in Oneida (oh-NYE-duh), Albany, Rensselaer (ren-suh-LEER), and Dutchess Counties. Gloversville and Johnstown became known for glove manufacturing. Buffalo was home to the first grain elevators, which made storing and shipping grain faster and easier. Buffalo became the world's largest grain port.

The Corning Flint Glass Works started in 1868. In 1886, Thomas Edison set up Edison Machine Works in Schenectady (skuh-NECK-tuh-dee). In 1892, this plant became the Edison General Electric Company. In 1888, George Eastman created the Kodak camera. In 1892, he started the Eastman Kodak Company in Rochester.

◄ This is a 1904 photo of the General Electric plant. The Kodak advertisement is from 1900. The original Kodak camera came with a roll of film in it. After taking all 100 pictures, the owner sent the camera to the Eastman Kodak Company where the film was developed. The photos and the camera (including new film) were then sent back to the owner.

Industrial Conditions

Workers in many early New York factories worked in terrible conditions. Early machines were often dangerous and could cause injuries or death. Cities with manufacturing centers became crowded. Children as young as eight years old worked twelve-hour shifts in hot and dirty factories. Thousands of children were sent to work in factories instead of going to school.

Some New York companies thought employee happiness was important. In the early 1900s, Eastman Kodak developed employee benefit programs. The Endicott-Johnson Shoe Company of Johnson City and Endicott was one of the first employers in America to give employees a share of the company's profits.

◀ By 1860, half of New York City's population was made up of immigrants, many of whom came looking for jobs. Hourly wages were low because immigrants needed work and were willing to take low-paying jobs. Slums—crowded areas where poverty and unhealthy living conditions are common—were filled with people who needed jobs. This photo is from 1912 and shows a slum on the Lower East Side of Manhattan.

A Better Life for Workers

Many New Yorkers helped to improve working conditions in America. A Jewish immigrant named Samuel Gompers organized the American Federation of Labor in 1886 and **united** workers throughout the nation. A woman named Fanny Wright was a member of the Workingmen's Party of New York City and led the fight for workers' rights and human equality.

By the early 1900s, laws were passed that limited or outlawed child labor. Labor **unions** were formed to protect workers from unfair business owners. New laws protected workers from losing earnings if an employer went out of business. These new laws improved working and living conditions for workers in New York City, New York state, and across the nation.

Glossary

acre (AY-kuhr) An area of land equal to 43,560 square feet.

immigrate (IH-muh-grayt) To move to a new country to make your home there.

industry (IN-duhs-tree) The production of goods, especially in a factory.

inland (IN-luhnd) Land that is away from the coast.

natural resource (NAH-chuh-ruhl REE-sohrs) Something found on the land or in the water that people can use.

plank (PLANK) A long, flat piece of sawed wood that is thicker than a board.

stock (STAHK) The shares owned in a company. When someone buys a company's stock, they own a part of the company and get a share of the company's profits.

stock market (STAHK MAR-ket) A place where shares of a stock are bought and sold.

transportation (tranz-puhr-TAY-shun) The movement of people or goods.

turnpike (TURN-pyke) A road that you have to pay to use.

union (YOON-yuhn) A group of workers who join together to protect their interests.

united (yoo-NIE-ted) Joined together as a single group.

Index

Primary Source List

Cover. Postcard of the Worcester Salt Factory, Silver Springs, New York. Ca. 1909. Rykoff Collection of Postcards.

Page 4. Engraved map of New Netherland. From a book of maps published around 1685 by Nicolaes Visscher II. Now in the New-York Historical Society.

Page 8. Philipsburg Manor. Established by Frederick Philipse in the early 1700s. Now a National Historic Landmark.

Page 10. *View of Wall Street from Corner of Broad.* Engraving from *Eighty Years' Progress of the United States*, published by L. Stebbins in 1869.

Page 12. *The Road Between New York and Bristol, Pennsylvania.* Engraving from Christopher Colles's *A Survey of the Roads of the United States of America*, 1789.

Page 12 (inset). Title page. From Christopher Colles's *A Survey of the Roads of the United States of America*, 1789.

Page 14. *View of Erie Canal.* Copy of watercolor by John William Hill, 1829. Original now in New York Public Library.

Page 14 (inset). Portrait of De Witt Clinton. Engraving, ca. 1825. This portrait also appears on U.S. $1,000 bills issued in 1880.

Page 16. De Witt Clinton locomotive. The locomotive made its first run on August 9, 1831. A wheel from the locomotive is now in the Smithsonian Institution. The photograph shown here is undated.

Page 16 (inset). Portrait of Robert Fulton. Painted by Charles Willson Peale, 1807.

Page 18. Inside Building 15, General Electric's Schenectady Works. Photograph taken 1904. Now in the Schenectady Museum.

Page 18 (inset). Advertisement for Kodak camera. Ca. 1900.

Page 20. Garment-making tenement, Elizabeth Street, Lower East Side, Manhattan. Photograph taken by Lewis Wickes Hine in March 1912.

Web Sites

Due to the changing nature of Internet links, The Rosen Publishing Group, Inc. has developed an on-line list of Web sites related to the subjects of this book. This site is updated regularly. Please use this link to access the list:

http://www.rcbmlinks.com/nysh/igny/